The History of BARGOED and GILFACH in photographs

Volume 1

by Paul James

This book is dedicated
to my late grandmother Mrs Annie Watkins.

Old Bakehouse Publications

Abertillery

First published in November 1996
Reprinted in February 1999

ISBN 1 874538 31 X

Published in the U.K. by
Old Bakehouse Publications
Church Street,
Abertillery, Gwent NP3 1EA
Telephone: 01495 212600 Fax: 01495 216222

Made and printed in the UK
by J.R. Davies (Printers) Ltd.

Foreword

by Councillor Harry A Andrews, J P

As we approach the final years of this century and await the dawn of a new millennium, this highly commendable book gives us an opportunity to travel back in time and witness the Bargoed enigma.

From a village to vibrant township, in a short space of time, brought about by the insatiable demands for the quality coal that had remained dormant for millions of years, waiting to offer its resource to a diverse workforce of artisans who would extract it for 80 years and create a society based on friendship and trust.

Bargoed and Gilfach like other valley communities developed as the demand for coal intensified throughout the world. The limited social hours available to the workforce were utilised to great effect. The creation of Educational, Cultural, Religious and Sporting institutions offered respite from the toil of the coalmine and Bargoed and Gilfach became busy centres of Trade and Commerce.

Calfaria, the Royal Hotel, New Hall Cinema and Cafe Ballroom are but a memory in Bargoed as was the loss of the Presbyterian and St Margaret's Church Hall in Gilfach. Central Hall, Hanbury Cinema and Hotel remain as a reminder of their days of social cohesion as they cry out for their lost dignity.

The present is for another day, the achievement of Paul James, who has encapsulated in these pages a vivid reminder of the past, and has presented an opportunity for the younger generation to ponder the future of Bargoed and Gilfach one hundred years after coal started to exert its influence on our community.

On your behalf I extend grateful thanks to Paul James for his dedication in creating this fascinating history of a community that was born from the quest for coal.

The hill is hard to climb, but the view is from the top!

Harry A Andrews.

Contents

Introduction

I have for many years been an enthusiastic collector of photographs of Bargoed, Gilfach and the surrounding district. After much thought, it occurred to me that the locality was in urgent need of a new photographic record of the area's rich history. Consequently I embarked on the project and this, my first publication, Bargoed and Gilfach in Photographs is the result which I hope will meet with full approval from its readers.

Records dating back to the 16th century indicate that Bargoed was a strictly rural parish. Industries were confined to agricultural varieties, with locally grown corn being ground in mills at both Bargoed and Gilfach. The rearing of sheep was another prime occupation, with a local woollen factory producing high quality cloth so that the people could have good home made products to wear. Farmers of the district led an important, strenuous but happy life yet not without some failings, it is said. They were much addicted to drink and loved to follow the hounds, but they were honest. Then came new industrial awakenings and greater prosperities to be unearthed. From a quiet rural obscure village, Bargoed through the 19th century rose to an enterprising and progressive town, being described as the 'Metropolis of the Rhymney Valley' and 'The City on the Hill'. The age of the coal industry had arrived and the acclaimed Powell Duffryn Steam Coal Company, founded in 1864, centred its investments in the Aberdare and Rhymney Valleys, Bargoed Colliery opening in 1897.

The new found wealth that heavier industries provided, soon attracted increased populations and social demands. A railway system was introduced to move coal and passengers, Bargoed School was opened in 1910 providing an education for all and the district was to be studded with churches and chapels. Included in this book are further photographs to remind us of yesteryear such as the Palace Cinema, the New Hall and the prestigious Bargoed Emporium.

My sincere thanks are extended to the many people of the area who have given me help in bringing this book to fruition and also to Mr Harry Andrews for providing the foreword. I am also particularly grateful to Mr Malcolm Thomas, author of a number of local books for his help and advice during the various stages of production.

Paul James

CHAPTER 1

Bargoed Town

1. Bargoed from the air with such landmarks as Trafalgar Square at the bottom centre and the sports field in the top left hand corner.

2. Once quite a focal point in the town of Bargoed and certainly well photographed was the renowned Emporium. This exceptionally early view is from around 1902 during a period of construction before the clock face had arrived. This was added in 1903.

3. A few years later, probably around 1908, the building is complete and to be noted is the clock which has now been added to the tower. The adjoining building immediately to the left is the old Welsh market.

4. A general view overlooking the town and to be seen prominently in the centre are the coolers for the former colliery. The former colliery site and surrounding area is being completely re-developed at the date of publication of this book, and a new by-pass is also planned.

5. The prolonged and severe winter of 1947 will no doubt revive a few memories for some readers of this book. The men are pictured here in Hanbury Road during a clean-up operation but unfortunately only one name of the 'shovellers' has been traced, that of Mr Howard Davies, who is second from the right.

6. To be seen here at Trafalgar Square is the war memorial in-situ and directly opposite is the old Hanbury Cinema with a valleys bus outside. Another once familiar sight in the background, is the conveyor belt transporting the waste from the colliery to the tip. The billboards advertising showings at the cinema, these days mark the site of the library.

7. As there was little or no traffic around in 1903, children could comfortably afford to pose for the cameraman in the middle of High Street. The scene here has changed considerably with the houses on the right being replaced by the Midland Bank and a food store etc. The buildings at the end of the left hand side of the street were demolished to make way for Bank Chambers.

8. A view looking towards Aberbargoed with the railway viaduct in the foreground which carries the Rhymney to Cardiff line, one of the few valley passenger rail services remaining in the South Wales valleys.

9. This view looking up Aberbargoed Hill reminds us once again of the many changes which have affected the district over the years. Gone is the old railway bridge and two once-popular public houses on the right, the Smith's Arms and the Greyhound. At the bottom of this photograph, on the right-hand side are the former houses of Riverside Row, since demolished. The road itself has now been completely straightened from its old twisting route.

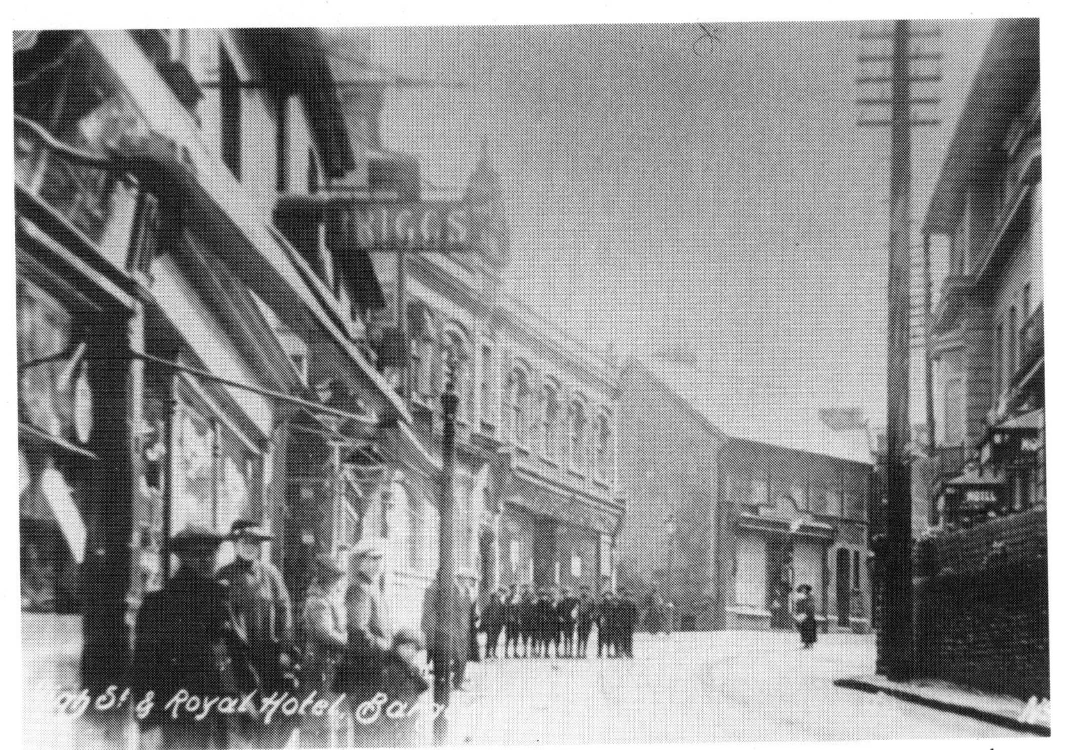

10. The High Street of Bargoed in about 1912. On the right-hand side of the street was the impressive Royal Hotel whilst on the opposite side can be seen the familiar sign of Brigg's shoe shop and a little further on is the site of Barclays Bank.

11. The lower end of High Street pictured some seventy years before this book was published. Seen on the right is Sam Ruther's fruit and veg shop which is now the premises of the Bradford and Bingley Building Society. The old pharmacy next door is now Boots Chemist. The ornate fronted building on the left is the old Palace Cinema.

12. A most interesting scene of the town before a hard road surface was needed and horse-drawn traffic was in fashion. In later years the well known shop of George, Rees and Jones occupied much of the left-hand side of the street whilst opposite, many readers may remember the old Palace Cinema which has yet to be built on this photograph.

13. Looking down Hanbury Road towards Trafalgar Square in 1908 with the Hanbury Hotel on the right. Also to be seen is a much frequented shop of years ago, that of Shibko the pawnbroker, whose motto was 'we lend money on a pin or a row of houses'.

14. The condition of the roughshod road surface indicates that this view of Hanbury Road is from around 1905. The gentleman on the left is stood in the doorway of Pritchard's cash chemist which these days, has been transformed into a fish and chip shop and an Indian restaurant. Notice the workmen on the right who are perched at the top of the poles installing early telegraph systems into the town.

15./16. Both of these photographs from 1959/1960 show the site clearance to make way for the building of the police houses by local builder Mr Sam Jones, in front of John Street. The trees on the left of Park Drive have since given way to the construction of new housing. In the photograph below can be seen the former ambulance station and some of the construction workers are Mr Tex Barry and Mr Alec Elliot.

17. Looking up Hanbury Road in 1927 and the road traffic is confined to a solitary car. Many of the shops here will have changed hands several times or disappeared altogether since this picture was taken. On the left is Hodges the gents outfitters which is now a shoe shop whilst on the corner on the opposite side of the road, today's shoppers will know this as a fruit and veg retailer.

18. A peaceful Hanbury Road in 1909 without a vehicle to be seen to disrupt the shoppers. A once familiar sight was the shop sun blind hanging over the pavements. In the distance can be seen Bank Chambers, built in 1906.

19. A superb aerial view of Bargoed taken during the 1950s showing a few former landmarks such as the old station, gas works and Junction Hotel.

20. From 1920 is this view of the Park and the Higher Elementary School as it was then called. The foreground seen in this picture is now a parking area.

21. Trafalgar Square in about 1956 with the former Post Office building on the left. In the foreground is the old wooden bus shelter, later to be removed en bloc and placed in the local park.

22. An industrial scene at Bargoed which is totally unrecognisable today. Gone are the colliery workings, the subsequent waste tips and the large gasometer in the foreground. Coal-produced gas lighting and cooking facilities were introduced to the area by the Bargoed Gas and Water Company in 1877. On the left can be seen the Greyhound Inn, once the home of Bargoed's world champion harpist William Morgan who won global recognition and praise at the end of the last century.

23. Factory Road and the railway viaduct as they appeared in 1952. The road has been improved somewhat since, now having two lanes beneath the arches. Aberbargoed is to be seen in the distance.

24. One of the earliest known photographs of Bargoed, taken towards the end of the 19th century. The centre of the town has yet to be fully developed and the new railway station is also awaiting construction.

25. From the 1950s is this view of Gilfach, before the building of the council housing estate. To be seen in the foreground are the mechanical buckets which were used for transporting coal waste from Britannia Colliery to the nearby tip.

26. It is not easy to compare this 1890s picture of High Street with that of today but for reference, the cottages on the right were to be demolished for the building of the Emporium and the impressive chapel building is that of Bethania. The tall building on the left is the town's oldest hotel, The Plas Newydd.

27. Aberbargoed Hill in 1905 with a road surface that leaves much to be desired. This picture shows the old railway bridge and pre-dates the building of the Greyhound Inn.

28. The Emporium, Pier Head Buildings was one of the most photographed landmarks in Bargoed town. This view is from about 1910 when the Emporium was establishing and advertising itself as 'the largest, best and cheapest ready-money drapery in the valley'.

29. The First World War ended in November 1918 and the country was swept with fervour to honour the dead. The crowds are gathered here at Trafalgar Square, Bargoed to witness the unveiling of the town's war memorial in the early 1920s.

30. Aberbargoed Hill in the early part of the 20th century with Bargoed Colliery in the background. This photograph was taken during the beginnings of the coal mining era as witnessed by the absence of the waste tip which was to build up toweringly over the years, as will be remembered by many readers.

31. Another photograph of a former Bargoed building, certain to revive a few memories is this one of the Junction Hotel taken in 1984.

32. The demise of the New Hall Cinema when it was destroyed by fire in February 1958, never to be re-built. Ironically the last film to be shown was 'Just My Luck' starring Norman Wisdom. Originally opened in 1908 as an entertainment hall, a few years before the arrival of the first silent films, the ground is now occupied by a Woolworth store.

33./34. Two interesting scenes of High Street with a number of former shops and buildings in view. Both of these photographs are from the 1950s and again reflect a picture of continual change. Below, the cottages on the left have now disappeared and also Calfaria Chapel, a little further along the street. Shoppers may also recall Longstaffs' Bazaar and The Emporium Shop.

35. The year is 1934 and work is well underway in constructing the new road diversion near Duffryn House. This dwelling, better known locally as The Puzzle House was built in about 1908. The photograph seen here shows on the left, the road to Brithdir whilst to the right lies the route to Bargoed, beneath the viaduct.

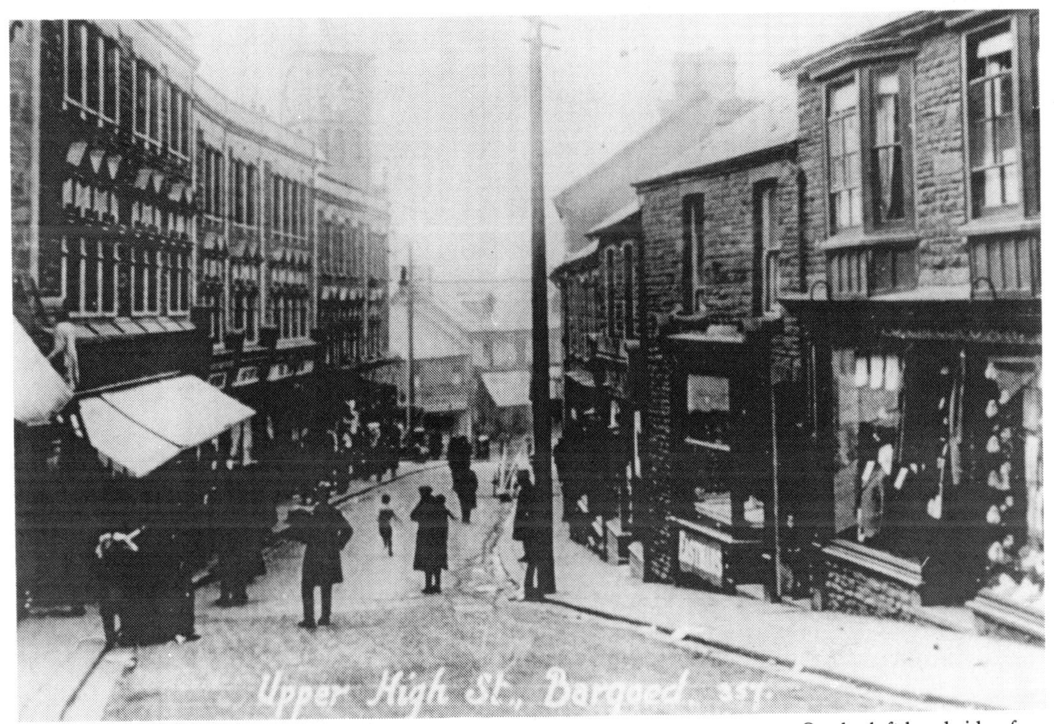

36. Upper High Street Bargoed as it would have looked some 80 years ago. On the left hand side of the street was the first Woolworth's store in the town, this now being the site of a car park.

37. A very elegant house which once graced Bargoed was Oakland Hall, seen here in about 1952. It was built by one Horace Davies who was probably better known as the 'Silver King', so named as he had the long standing reputation of paying his employees in silver! In latter years, readers may well remember the local family solicitors, Mr and Mrs Withers occupying the house until the 1980s. Unfortunately this once opulent old building was demolished on the 20th April 1993.

38. Probably one of the oldest photographs in this Bargoed book is this one, taken during the 1880s of a local thatch-roofed cottage. It has not been possible to establish precisely who the ladies and gentleman are here, but the cottage was at one time occupied by Evan and Rachel Thomas and their children. This very old building was demolished in about 1910 to make way for St Gwlady's Church Hall.

39. Commercial Street Gilfach during the 1950s, a much quieter scene when this particular picture was taken. Local inhabitants will remember a few of the shops here, such as Dan Thomas (Greengrocer), Fred Lucas (Butcher), Sam Jones (Fruiterer) and Ken Caesar (Chemist).

40. Looking up the main road from Gilfach to Bargoed. The shop seen on the corner, left hand side may be remembered by some as Ziraschi's Fish and Chip Shop. Whilst on the opposite side was Ruther's Fruit and Veg and Shute the Butcher's. Beneath this part of the road once ran the tramway from Gilfach Colliery.

41. A look at St Anne's Crescent in the days when the area was faced with the eyesore of a waste tip. Thankfully, that tip has now been dispersed and replaced with park land. This picture dates from the 1920s.

42. The War Memorial of Bargoed on its original site in Trafalgar Square. This monument was erected to honour the fallen of Bargoed and district who gave their lives for King and Country during the First World War 1914-1918. In later years it was removed and re-sited to its present position in the Park.

43. A photograph overlooking a once busy railway system. The wagons at the bottom of the picture are on the line which ran upwards to the village of Fochriw and onwards to Brecon whilst the viaduct carries the main line from Cardiff to Rhymney and eventual connection with the Merthyr, Tredegar and Abergavenny track. In the background is the former Aberbargoed Station serving the Brecon and Merthyr line (Rhymney branch).

44. Looking up Wood Street many years before publication of this Bargoed book. Two prominent buildings to be seen on the right are the old Hanbury Cinema and Post Office, whilst to the left of the road, the Methodist Central Hall has yet to be built.

45./46. Both of these photographs help illustrate the detrimental effect that the old coal waste tips once had on the local environment. Above, is Gilfach School, the land in front of which is now the Park and bowling green. In the lower photograph, St Annes Crescent is surrounded by rough terrain which these days has been reclaimed and now houses the tennis courts.

CHAPTER 2

Trade, Industry and Transport

47. Bowen's General Store at 30 West Street, Bargoed during the 1920s. Outside the shop are Mrs E Bowen, Mr Ivor Bowen with the trilby hat and a young Mr Dobson. Regrettably it has not been possible to trace the name of the lady assistant.

48. Mr Ivor Bowen selling his provisions from his horse and cart in South Street. If there are some readers who can recall this door to door service, can they also remember the name of the horse?
(It was Lightning!)

49. The Walters family stand outside their shop in Gwerthonor Place during the 1930s. Seen left to right here are William, Brian, Lewis and Margaret with assistant Beryl Oates and Herbert Walters by the delivery van.

Don't Forget

∵ A. SHIBKO,

PAWNBROKER,

33, Hanbury Road, Bargoed,

Lends Money on a Pin or a Row of Houses, or on Note of Hand at 27, Charles Street Cardiff.

UTMOST SECRECY OBSERVED.

DON'T FORGET THE OLD FIRM!

50. The staff and waitresses dressed in Art Deco style uniforms outside the Hall Cafe which was attached to the Hall Cinema. This was quite a large cafe which could accommodate more than 200 customers and was owned by a Mr Lewis who was always referred to locally as 'Lewis A1'.

51. Stan Hughes' Garage at Gilfach Street Bargoed. The photograph dates from 1938 and the style and prices of the cars in the showroom make interesting reading. Stan Hughes is seen standing in the doorway surrounded by his staff.

52. In the 1920s, Mr T Morris poses alongside one of the Powell Duffryn lorries at the colliery. To the Powell Duffryn Company must be attributed the responsibility for the growth and development, that transformed Bargoed and the surrounding district at the turn of the last century, from sparsely populated rural communities to important industrial regions.

53. A picture which is some 80 years old shows the staff and probably their own delivery cart of Dan Thomas' grocery shop. This was a family-owned business which traded in Commercial Street Gilfach for many years.

54. The 'Gwalia' van of Mr A R Williams, Bargoed. Unfortunately, little is known of the origins of this particular photograph but possibly it is one of the town's early furniture removal wagons pictured in about 1905.

55. In 1930 can be seen Miss Kitty Chinnock and Mr Billy Pember on their rounds in the Avenue, Gilfach. The cart, loaded with fresh fruit and vegetables for delivery to the customers' doors is being hauled by the faithful horse 'Mag'.

56. A picture, taking the reader back to the days when Bargoed afforded a hotel of such splendour as the Royal. Changing times forced closure and subsequent demolition during the 1960s to be replaced by a supermarket etc.

JOHN WILLIAMS,

(Late MAITLAND)

47A HEOLDDU ROAD, BARGOED.

UNDERTAKER,

Complete Funeral Furnisher,

AND DIRECTOR.

Personal Supervision to all Orders.

Cheapest and Best Firm in the Valley !

TEL. P.O. 59.

EWART E. PHILLIPS

ACCOUNTANT,

HOUSE AGENT & INSURANCE BROKER.

. CENTRAL CHAMBERS, .

HIGH STREET, BARGOED.

Prompt Settlements Ensured.

57. Mr Richard Walters who was probably better known to many locals as 'Dickie Flagon', is seen outside his shop in Gilfach. This was a well known family business in the area for many years.

58. This is how public transport in the Bargoed area used to look, with the bus crew pausing for a moment during the 1930s.

59. Caught on film during the 1980s and just prior to demolition is Clarks Cornstore whilst next door Bethania Chapel is already seen at the hands of the dismantlers. The site is upper High Street and now a car parking area.

60. No.12 Vere Street as it looked during the 1930s when it was a popular Gilfach general store. Stood outside are Elizabeth, Kitty and William Chinnock. The shop is now converted into a private dwelling.

61. The staff of Messrs George, Rees and Jones at an annual function in 1947. The three gentlemen seated centre front are the owners of the former Bargoed shop and left to right are Mr Jones, Mr George and Mr Rees.

62. It must be many years since such a scene was witnessed outside a Bargoed shop. The queue here is pictured outside George, Rees and Jones Ltd. one morning in the late 1940s waiting for the doors to open on the first day of a grand sale.

63. Dozens of faces waiting to be identified by readers of this Bargoed book. The photograph was taken at a George, Rees and Jones staff social evening of 1952.

64. Members of the Conti family pictured during the early 1920s as evidenced for instance by the model of the car with its solid rubber tyres. This Italian family were proprietors of the Continental Cafe which was in Hanbury Road opposite the site of today's Police Court.

65. The Gwerthonor Hotel is still to be seen in Commercial Street, Gilfach but, this is how it appeared in about 1910 with a fleet of horses and drays on the road. Sat on the cart on the far right is a local personality, Mr R M Walters or 'Dickie Flagon' as he was better known.

66. The Square Cafe as seen in 1948 although readers will note that the frontage has changed a little since. One of the oldest surviving family businesses in Bargoed, it has been in the Ricci family since 1929.

67. Inside the cafe, again in 1948, a visiting army band takes a lunch break. Standing in the doorway, at the back of the picture is Mr Luigi Ricci the cafe owner who ventured with his family from Bardi in Italy in 1908.

68. The Powell Duffryn Colliery, a once famous landmark in the district. The building in the foreground is the washery with the housecoal shaft on the far right.

69./70. Two interesting scenes at the colliery in 1956. On the left is the washery and on the right is the bucket line from Britannia Colliery to Bargoed. To give today's reader an idea of the location, in the distance can be seen Brithdir Cemetery.

71. Looking north, another view shows the settling tower on the left adjacent to the washery.

72./73. Two contrasting views of the colliery. Bargoed Colliery was originally owned by the Powell Duffryn Steam Coal Company, the first shaft being sunk in 1897. Two separate shafts were used to extract the high quality steam coal and at its peak during the First World War more than 2100 men were employed at the workings. A third shaft was completed in 1903 to reach the nearby seam of house coal, so rich were the coal pickings in those days. Above can be seen the conveyor carrying the waste to the ever rising tip with the coolers and power house below.

74. In the foreground lies Brithdir Pit also to be known as 'Bargoed Housecoal'. The extraction of coal came to an end here in 1949 but the mine was used for many years after as a training school for would-be colliers.

75. The crane by the river is seen removing coal spill and this is the area where the Ryan Company began their extraction business in 1950. The ash tips on the left and centre have since been completely landscaped and the old Bargoed Colliery tip is to be seen in the distance.

76. As tradition had it, it was customary for sons to follow fathers and so on into the mining industry in days gone by, as often this would be the only source of work in the Welsh valleys. Seen here in about 1920 at Bargoed is Mr Alfred Shears and his son Reginald.

77. A group of Bargoed Colliery workers including banksmen, pitmen, labourers and the winding man. It was here at the South Downcast Shaft in 1909 that a World Record of 4020 tons of coal was extracted in a single working shift.

78. Cartwrights Colliery at Gilfach in 1917. This was situated near Gwerthonor Ganol Farm.

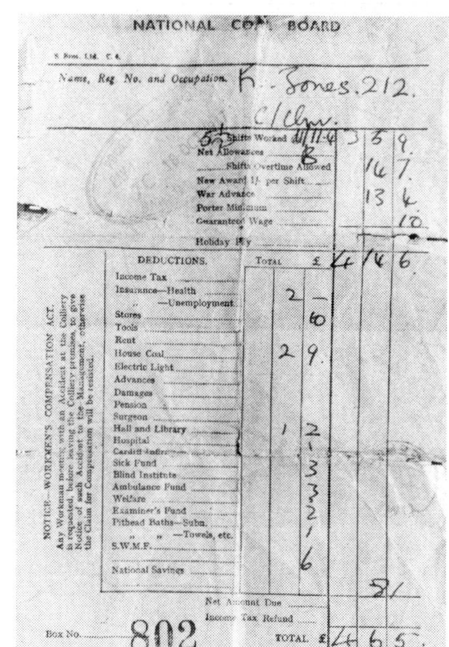

NATIONAL CO[illegible] BOARD

Name, Reg. No. and Occupation K. Jones. 212. C/Clnr.

	£	s.	d.
5½ Shifts Worked 4/11/4[illegible]		3 5	9.
Net Allowances 8			
...... Shifts Overtime Allowed		16	7.
New Award 1/- per Shift			
War Advance		13	4
Porter Minimum			
Guaranteed Wage			10
Holiday Pay			
TOTAL	4	14	6.

DEDUCTIONS.	s.	d.
Income Tax		
Insurance—Health	2	—
„ —Unemployment		
Stores		10
Tools		
Rent		
House Coal	2	9.
Electric Light		
Advances		
Damages		
Pension		
Surgeon		
Hall and Library	1	2
Hospital		1
Cardiff Infirmary		
Sick Fund		3
Blind Institute		3
Ambulance Fund		2
Welfare		1
Examiner's Fund		
Pithead Baths—Subn.		
„ „ —Towels, etc.		
S.W.M.F.		6
National Savings		

Net Amount Due

Income Tax Refund

Box No. 802 TOTAL £ 4 6 5.

NOTICE—WORKMEN'S COMPENSATION ACT. Any Workman meeting with an Accident at the Colliery is requested, before leaving the Colliery premises, to give Notice of such Accident to the Management, otherwise the Claim for Compensation will be resisted.

79. The sheer expanse of Bargoed Colliery meant that it was very much self-contained and supporting, generating its own electrical and pneumatic power etc. This picture from 1956 shows the coke ovens on the south side.

80./81. The Rhymney Valley was swarmed with coal workings for almost one hundred years, beginning in the middle of the 19th century. Gilfach contributed to the industrial wealth of the district with a colliery extracting quality coal. The site was near to where Andrews Close is today and these photographs depict the scene as it appeared in the early 1900s.

82./83. After the First World War ended in 1918, normality returned with the hope that industrial and transport systems would expand rapidly once again. There was an urgent need for a new road and bridge over the Rhymney Valley line and a cameraman from about 1919 has captured some local men employed on the project.

84. The coal industry was fraught with workers unrest on numerous occasions over the years and for many genuine reasons, particularly in the early years of growth and unscrupulous employers. Above is a picture at Bargoed during the Great Strike of 1912 and the men are seen scouring the surface for coal waste to burn in their fires during the dispute. The Great Strike of 1912 started in the Derbyshire coalfield on February 26th and within three days, three-quarters of a million men were out. The dispute lasted until April 8th by which time the Liberal Government were forced to intervene by way of introducing the minimum wage bill, thus forcing the coal owners to concede.

85. Bystanders watch as the delicate task of lifting a footbridge alongside the existing bridge at Commercial Street and Gwerthonor Place during the 1950s.

86. Looking south down the platforms of Bargoed Station. This is a very early photograph which was taken before the building of the new booking office. The old fashioned gas lamp and trolley will evoke a few memories of rail travel in the days of steam and station atmosphere.

87. Another view of the station, this time facing north and presenting a different sight compared with today's single platform. The Rhymney and Cardiff trains would stop on the lines at the right of this picture, whilst the seat on the opposite platform is where passengers would await their train to Fochriw and all stations to Brecon.

88. The halcyon days of steam power are recorded here with a freight train having passed over the viaduct and a passenger train heads in the opposite direction towards picturesque Breconshire. Notice the large water storage tank at the end of the platform where the locomotives would stop to refill.

89. This photograph which may have been taken from the viaduct shows Factory Road which has seen substantial improvements since this scene from about 1955.

90. These days there are enthusiasts who will marvel at the sight of a steam train, yet its smoke, noise and smuts of burnt coal were considered a nuisance in the valleys before the arrival of diesel powered units in the late 1950s. The freight train seen here is being hauled by an 0-6-2 Class 56 locomotive on the Newport to Brecon line, behind Factory Road.

91. An unusual photograph of a passenger train as it approaches the station on the line from Rhymney to Cardiff. There are a few notable changes to the road on the left, the chapel is now the site of a garage and of course the Junction Hotel is no longer there.

92. Thankfully the old coal tips which were valley eyesores for many years, have now disappeared. Here we see the tip being removed from St. Annes Crescent in 1947 preparing the ground for the Park which was developed some years later.

93. Further evidence of the improvements made to waste land and the environment in recent years. This is the lane at the rear of the Capel Hotel, Gilfach as it looked in 1952. Also to be seen are the Bargoed Colliery coolers.

94. From the days of the Gelligaer Urban District Council bus service, is seen this 1930s Leyland coach parked at the depot in Aeron Place, Gilfach.

95. Looking towards Aberbargoed from the railway station, one is reminded of yet more prominent buildings which have since disappeared, including the Smith's Arms Hotel seen in the centre.

CHAPTER 3

Churches, Chapels and Schools

96. A glance at High Street Bargoed in 1908 will serve to remind readers of Calfaria Chapel which once stood here. The chapel, since demolished is now the site of a clothing store.

97. Walking along Park Place, Gilfach are the worshippers of St. Margaret's church during a one-time traditional Whitsun march in the 1930s.

98. The Salvation Army was founded in 1865 and has since become a worldwide organisation. This is the Bargoed S A Band pictured in 1911 with Bandmaster Harry Bosanko. The Citadel these days is in Greenfield Street.

99. Members of Bethania Welsh Calvinistic Methodist Church enjoying their Whitsun walk-out during the 1930s, passing the Police Station.

100. The once familiar landmark of Bethania Chapel which stood at Upper High Street. This place of worship was built in 1877 and saw a life span of one hundred and five years before closure in 1982. The building fell into decay and was demolished in 1985 and the site now forms part of a car park.

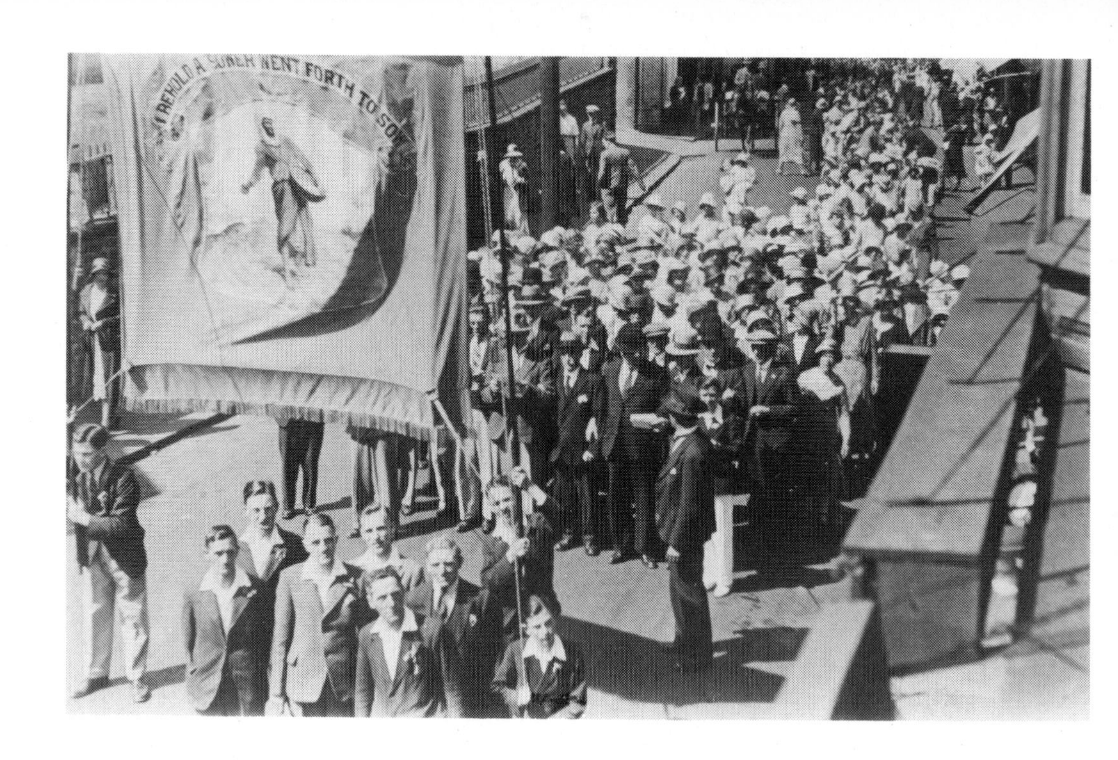

101/102. The processions of religious fervour continue here in another two photographs. The crowds above represent the congregation of Bargoed Methodist Church whilst below can be seen the ladies and gentlemen of Hanbury Road Baptist during Whitsun 1958.

103. Hanbury Road Baptist Church

Until the latter half of the 19th century, Welsh was the predominant tongue in the chapels of Bargoed and the valley, with resistance to anything else most forceful. Sustained immigration of English-speaking workers to the industrial areas of South Wales however, was to bring about an unstopable demand for changes in attitudes amongst the non-conformist believers. The first English Baptist movement was started in Bargoed as early as 1877 although many, despite their lack of knowledge of the Welsh language, continued their worship at Caersalem Welsh Baptist Church on the Aberbargoed side of the valley. Seeing Bargoed itself, as a target for an English speaking church, followers of the faith began holding meetings in private dwellings, pioneered by one John Llewellyn, an inspector for the Rhymney Railway Company. At such a meeting, held in August 1896 at the house of Mr and Mrs W H Jones, High Street, it was formerly agreed that the English speaking cause should now endeavour to form their own Church and Sunday School. This was not an easy task and there being no other building available at the time, the members managed to lease the assembly room adjacent to the Plasnewydd Hotel, rent free for one year. The church was officially constituted here in November 1896 and the flock grew loud and strong, so much so that they were accepted into the Monmouthshire Baptist Association the following year. Soon, the yearning for a house of worship gathered momentum and in June 1897, the Hanbury Estate of Pontypool agreed to lease a plot of land in Hanbury Road, Bargoed for the building of a place of worship. Despite acceptance of the architect's plans, only the schoolroom in the basement of the buildings was constructed, opening in 1899 and serving the purpose for another seven years. By this time financial conditions had improved and the chapel was completed to its original plans with capacity for almost one thousand worshippers, officially opening in 1906. Thereafter, years of hard work and dedication by the members enabled the building loans to be paid off by 1941. The first pastor at Hanbury Road was Rev Harri Edwards from Abercarn who served for 19 years, whilst today the church is in the careful hands of Rev Terence Casey.

104. Rev Harri Edwards

105. The Deacons of Hanbury Road Chapel, photographed with their minister in 1942. Seen left to right are, standing - Mr D S Jones, Mr D J Jones, Mr H D Riden (well known photographer), Mr F J Hollow, Mr C Leonard and Mr W J Rees. Seated - Mr W F Howard (Gilfach ironmonger), Mr H Roberts, Mr D Williams, Rev W E Mathias-Williams, Mr J Williams, Mr A Baber (Blackwood shop proprietor) and Mr F Astin (Secretary). Inset is Mr H J Morgan (Church Treasurer).

106. Again, seen passing the Police Station is this parade of worshippers from Hanbury Road English Baptist Chapel on a Whitsun march through the town.

107./108. St Gwlady's Church was constructed and opened for worship in 1876 with new extensions added in 1893. The photograph above is very early, probably around 1890. Below is a later photograph showing completion of the extensions but the roadway still has to be properly developed and surfaced.

109. A congregation of mainly local pensioners are seen here inside the Presbyterian Church, Gilfach probably during the late 1940s. Many familiar faces to be recognised but in the front row are - Mr Ernie Maund, Mr Gunning (Minister), 'Tommy Dancer', 'Aunty Biddy' (Post Office), and Mr Scandrett the hairdresser.

110. An industrious scene at the old Gilfach quarry with religious connections. It was from this quarry, which was situated near the Gilfach Bowling Green that stone was hacked to build the Presbyterian Chapel. The Gwerthonor Hotel was also constructed with materials from the site.

111. The former Presbyterian Chapel in Commercial Street Gilfach. This chapel was built between 1904 and 1905 during a great period of religious revival which was sweeping across Wales, and is pictured here shortly after the official opening. With continued interests other than religion, the congregations diminished until final closure and demolition in August 1995. The site was reconstituted and a 'Garden of Peace' was constructed and opened on St David's Day 1996.

112. A wintry scene taken at the St Margarets Church Hall, the hall being demolished in September 1988.

113. The South Bargoed Junior Boys School in about 1960. Standing at the rear left is Mr Williams and on the right, fellow staff member Stuart Burrows. Stuart of course went on to win international acclaim as a distinguished opera star.

114. South Bargoed Junior Boys again photographed in the school yard during the 1960s. The teacher on this occasion is Mr Meade.

115. Bargoed South Girls School Scholarship Class in 1940. Back row, left to right - Megan Lucas, Aileen Beard, Ira Stephens, Ira Smallman, Margaret Yeoman, unknown, Barbara Morgan, Maureen James, Marion Llewellyn, Mavis Smalley, Eira Weale, Betty Williams and Edna Davies. Middle row - Margaret Stephens, Eileen Driscol, Barbara Powell, Lillian Vallis, Ethney Williams, Miss Alice Davies (Teacher), Beryl Evans, Connie Taswell, unknown, unknown and Nellie Marsh. Front row - Violet Jones, Pat Ellis, Beryl Morris, Betty Jacobson, Mair Jones, Naomi Rook, Betty Wilcox, unknown, Sally Bartlett, Eileen Jones, Sheila Williams, Margaret Edwards and Margaret Bull.

116. The Higher Elementary School Bargoed as it was originally known, first opened in February 1910. The school was managed by a team of local ministers of religion and councillors, catering for specially selected post-primary pupils before secondary education was guaranteed for all in 1920. The first headmaster was Mr Sylvan Evans.

117. School staff in 1960. Standing, left to right - Messrs. M Burtch BA, LRAM (Music), W A Ryan BA (English and Dramatics), H Murray BSc (Maths and General Science), R J Porter BSc (Chemistry), J Morris BSc (Geography and Geology), R Davies BA (Welsh and History), C H Howell ATD (Art and School Film), A R Price C & G (Metalwork and Engineering Drawing), I Thomas BSc (Maths and Geography), Keri Edwards BA (English and School Magazine), G M Phillips BSc (Maths and School Accounts), J C Evans Bsc (Physics), P G Williams (Physical Education), T T Edwards, BA PhD (French). Seated - Mrs K Lewis MA (French), Mrs L Davies BA (Welsh), Miss E M Jones BSc (Biology, Botany and Zoology), Mr W R D Jones BA, BSc (History and Economics), Mr A Shone C & G (Deputy Headmaster and Handicraft), Mr W Haydn Davies MA (Headmaster), Mrs M A Hughes (Senior Mistress/Domestic Science), Mrs E P Walters (Physical Education), Miss Morwen Davies BA (Latin), Miss B Hugh BA (Religious Instruction and French), Mrs M Hamer (School Secretary).

118. Non-Teaching Staff 1960 with the headmaster. Back row, left to right - Mr Baden Morgan, Mrs Ruth Williams, Mrs Ivy Prosser, Mrs Eira Beale, Mrs Glenys Gibson, Miss Doris Nelsen and Mr Leonard Jenkins. Front row - Mrs Mary E Uzzell, Mrs Megan Hamer, Mr W H Davies MA, Miss Blanche Gibson and Mrs Mary E Williams.

119. The pupils and two of the teachers of Bargoed South Junior School pose for a photograph in the school yard. The teachers are Mr T Jones and Mr Borret.

120. Gilfach Fargoed Junior School in 1969. Back row, left to right - M L Jones, H Noakes, K Jones, P Tasker, S Williams, E Griffiths, S Cox, A L Wallbank, A Powell and H Foster. Middle row - unknown, N Perks, D Thomas, R Lewis, J Kallend, S Maslin, J Howells, R Bevan, R Viles, S Marshall and C James. Front row - K Baker, L Mathews, J Spearman, L MaCarthy, Mrs Edwards (Teacher), J Oliver, unknown, K Heenan and J Williams.

121. Some teachers and pupils at Bargoed Grammar School in 1968. Unfortunately it has not been possible to identify the pupils but the staff seated at the front are left to right - Mr J Morris, Mr A Shone, Mr K Edwards (Headmaster) and Mrs E Walters.

122. St David's Day provides an annual opportunity for the local children to dress in national Welsh costume. This picture was taken at Bargoed Infants School on 1st March 1982 and amongst those to be seen left to right are - Christopher Bird, Russell Melins, Craig Leheigh, Stephen Evans, Geraint Bodman, Jennifer Williams, Emma Lewis, Emma Jones, Charlene James, Cher Butcher, Corrine Stokes, Tina Carpenter, Corrina Stokes, Kelly Couzens, Gemma Rowlands, Janine Bird, Georgina Ryder, Maria Rees and Michelle Lewis.

123. The girls of Gilfach Infants' School with their teacher Miss Watkins. The picture dates from 1928 so the young ladies seen here would now be in their seventies, some names have been traced and these are Cora Watkins, Esme Mathews, Olga Morgan, Edith Flew, Gwyneth Williams, Phylis Laye, Megan Chappel, Ceridwen Lambert, Glenys Nicholas, Anna Young, Kate Mathews, Dulcie Pickwick, Olga Davies and Peggy Morris.

124. Gilfach Fargoed Boys School in the early 1920s. The boys are pictured with two of their teachers at the time, Miss D Davies, on the left and far right is Miss M Leyshon.

125. In slightly more modern times, thought to be in 1960, is this group of boys and girls at Gilfach Infants School. The teacher standing far left will be remembered as Miss Davies. Some of the pupils are Gareth Lewis, Dawn Singer, Susan Budd, Peter Dando and Steven Court.

126. Vere Street Infants School at Gilfach and the mode of school dress seen here will evoke a few memories.

127. This school photograph of Gilfach Fargoed Boys' School is approximately seventy years old, thus unfortunately the only name available at the time of publication of this book is that of the teacher seen on the right who is Mr Emlyn Williams.

128. The soccer team of Gilfach Boys' School pose for a photograph at Christmas 1921 to mark their achievement of being the Rhymney Valley League leaders. The names of four of the teachers present have been traced and they are, starting second from the left, Mr E Williams, Mr T C Jones (Headmaster), Mr Garnet and Mr Jim Watkins. Regrettably the name of the gentleman on the far left and not been determined.

129. Again the pupils and staff of 'Gilfach Boys' stop for a photo session, this time during the 1950s. The teachers are Mr Jack Wade, left and Mr Amwell Jones right. Many of the boys' names are known and apologies are extended to those omitted. Left to right are, back row - K Lewis, unknown, M Knight, R Sharp, A Thorley, unknown, R Hollifield and K Tucker. Middle row - A Meek, L Richards, D Pugh, S Walters, N Brooks, J Walters, J Ashcroft, unknown, R Mullett and J Spiker. Front row - P Thomas, unknown, unknown, unknown, J Trew, D Richards, J Jones, T Basham, E Jones and J Coles.

130. St David's Day 1970 and some of the pupils of Gilfach Infants' School seen here are, back row - Alison Hughes, unknown, Maxine Henderson, Robert Flannagan, unknown, John Whelan, Helen Jones and Gary Evans. Third row - Denise Blow, Mandy Higgs, Caroline James, unknown, Gavin Cushing, unknown and Alan Faulkner. Second row - David Viles, Jane Wooldridge, unknown, Brian Jones, Ian Watts and Wendy Waters. Front row - Phillip Diamond, Susan Lewis, Carl Langford, Susan Jones and David Lewis.

131. Another picture at Gilfach Infants', this time in 1973. Back row, left to right - Mrs Bevan (Teacher), unknown, Mark Francis, Lee Coopey, Karl James, Hugh Thomas, Mark Owen, Alan Hawkins and Mrs Evans (Teacher). Middle row - Lyndon Cross, Lisa Maund, Michael Greenaway, Margaret Morgan, Michael Barnett, Carolyn Pugh and Philip Davies. Front row - Charlene Bye, Elizabeth Shorey, Ceri Thomas, Barbara Lynch, Anita Ellis, Jacqueline James and Helen Richards.

132. A traditional school photograph from Gilfach Boys. Perhaps former pupils will be able to recognise themselves here and remember Mr Thomas who is standing on the right. Some of the boys seen are - Ceri Price, J Walters, David Richards, Malcolm Knight, Tommy Basham, Jimmy Trew, A Thorley, Robert Sharp, Julian Jones and David Thomas.

133. Gilfach Infants School 1960. Back row, left to right - Ms Kitty Edwards, unknown, Robert Williams, Alan Shaw, Malcolm Hill, unknown, unknown, Alan Davies, unknown and John Morris. Third row - Alan Harris, Lynne Davies, unknown, Linda Davies, unknown, Peggy Clothier, Ann Cushion, Jocelyn Parry, unknown, unknown and Alex Guzvic. Second row - Gaynor Stewart, unknown, Susan Howells, Alison Evans, Sandra Bruton, Karen Beale, Mary Evans, Jane Hollifield, Joanne Rice, Linda Gardener and unknown. Front row - Lawson Evans, Gareth Thorley, Lawrence Evans, Terry Chard and unknown.

134. Another chance to remember some more familiar faces from Gilfach Fargoed Boys School with teachers Mr Jack Wade and Mr Emlyn Williams.

135. An opportunity for a class from the Gilfach Infants School to be photographed in 1963. Seen with the youngsters are Ms Woodyatt on the left and Mrs Jones on the far right. The pupils include H Foster, Mark Barry, Julie Davies, Linda McCarthy, Haydn Noaks, Sandra Pickering, Julie Hurst, Robert Lewis, Michael Jones. Martin Willets and Andrew Wallbank.

136. From the mid 1950s is seen a class at Gilfach Boys' with teacher Mr Jim Watkins. The pupils seen left to right are, back row - M Jenkins, H Horton, P Thomas, L Davies, L Williams, M Davies, R Courts and R Mullett. Middle row - D Turner, D Davies, R Hollifield, L Richards, J Evans, D Gough, J Cox and D Calvert. Front row - Bryn Whittal, C Payne, F Jenner, J Ashcroft, K Lewis, A Meek and S Walters.

137. Bargoed Grammar School 1st XV rugby team season 1970-71. Back row, left to right - R Davies, J Mathews, A Mullins, D Gordon, B Cockram, G Jones and N Walbyoff. Middle row - D Williams, M Hughes, A Terry, G Rees, M Grabowski, B Evans, G Watkin, M Scanlon and A Hurd. Front row - B Morgan, D Watkins, P Patterson, Mr M J Vincent, M Pratten, Mr K Edwards MA, G Williams, L Scanlon and F Grist.

CHAPTER 4

People and Events

138. Local 'Jazz Bands' have for a long time enjoyed a dedicated following. On the left is to be seen David Langford, mascot of the 'Flits' pictured in 1948.

The Event of the Year !!

Look Out for

Bargoed May-Day Show

MAY, 1912.

FOR ALL PARTICULARS APPLY—

E. G. STAPLETON, Secretary,

14, Wood Street, BARGOED.

139. The Gilfach Flits Jazz Band pictured during a day of celebration at the top of Vere Street. The year is 1948 and the band has been proclaimed champions of Great Britain.

140. The cast of Bethania Church Sunday School's pantomime Sian-r-Siôn, Jack and Jill in 1936. Seated far left is Mrs Margaret Boobyer and on the right is Miss Beryl Williams. Amongst the many players to be seen are, Olwen Evans, John Strange, David Jones, Hilda Price, Emrys Williams and Beryl Morris.

141. The Jazz Band leads the procession of the 1978 carnival through Gwerthonor Place, Gilfach.

142. A massed band of gentlemen calling themselves the Gilfach Page Boys Carnival Band during the 1930s. This photograph was taken outside the old Bargoed Hall which still stands with a new doctors' surgery having been built alongside.

143. British Legion members Gilfach Street Bargoed in the 1920s. The building later became the ex-servicemens club which is now the home of Bargoed Rugby Club. Names have been given for some of the faces and these are Mrs T D Evans, Margaret Gallaven, Mrs Bussell, Mrs Ted Jones, Mrs Jennet Gale, Mrs Clarke and Mrs Strange.

144. The residents of Usk Road at a 'Street Party' during the 1930s either for the Silver Jubilee of 1935 or the Coronation of 1937 and some of the names to be seen here are Jacky Langford, Mrs Vowles, Mrs Ecket, H Griffiths, Barbara Lea, Jack Weaver, Liza Weaver, Bessie James, Alice Langford, Gwen Smart, Kenny Conway, Charlie Conway, Billy Williams, Bert Langford, Howard Bowen, Sid Kirby, Elizabeth Jenkins and Harry Mortimer.

145. Another well-attended photo session, this time at Llewellyn Street and among those to be seen are - Mrs Griffin, Dolly Carter, Hazel Rice, Doreen Rice, Brynley Oliver, Muriel Pugh, Brian Ashcroft, Colin Hancox, Gaynor Rice, Florrie Thomas, Haydn Ashcroft, Gwyneth Jenner, Marion Bradbury, Beryl Butland, Jean Jenner, Shirley Pugh, Lynne Davies, Mavis Butland, June Pugh, Christine Rice, Tony Maund, Doreen Speicher, Melita Davies, Frank Jenner, Jack Ashcroft, Margaret Weaver, Rene Davies, Ted Oliver and Bronwen Blewitt.

146. A group of Trinity Chapel players are seen on stage at the Institute in about 1937 following their performance of 'Ali Baba and the Forty Thieves'.

147. The 1st Bargoed Scout Troop at St Gwladys Church in 1937. Back row, left to right - Bob Smith and Douglas Mustoe. Third row - G Davies, R Fox, M Williams, R Groom, M Yates, K Rees, R Hurcombe, unknown, B Mustoe, unknown, unknown and D Yates. Second row - Rev David Evans, George Cornwall (Scout Master), Mrs Scott (Barclays Bank), C Conway, Rev Christmas Griffiths, K Conway, M Jones, R Flowers, R Bryant and W Boobyer.

148. A rare surviving photograph which was taken at McDonnel Road Bargoed in August 1902 during celebrations to mark the Coronation of King Edward VII. In the backround, to the right can be seen Heolddu Isaf Farm originally known as Pen-yr-Heol-Ddu.

149. Ysgol Cwmraeg, the Welsh School is the venue in 1970 for the parents displaying their ornamental headress at the Easter Bonnet Parade.

150. The Gilfach Page Boys Jazz Band stand in Heolddu Road, Bargoed in 1932. Heolddu Road was originally called Wingfield Road after a former colliery with the same name on Bargoed mountain.

151. A jolly boys and girls outing from Gilfach Workman's Club. The exact location of the trip is unknown but it is thought to be during the 1930s and no doubt there will be a reader somewhere who can recall the event and know a few of the faces seen here.

152. This is a local childrens' Christmas party which was held at the Ambulance Hall, John Street, Bargoed by RAFA Club members and dates from the 1960s.

153. Bargoed Male Voice Choir with a lady accompanist are photographed outside Bargoed Hall in the year 1926. Unfortunately it has not been possible to identify any names other than those of Mr J Morris, Mr J Rowlands and Mr Kedward.

154. Bargoed Special Police attending an annual dinner during the 1940s and to be seen standing at the rear centre is Mr Folland the superintendent.

155. Some members and guests of the formidable Gelligaer Historical Society are pictured at their 21st Anniversary Celebration in 1982 and among those to be seen are Mr Harry Andrews (Chairman of the Council), Mrs Doreen Andrews, Christopher Jones-Jenkins (Treasurer), Haydn Davies (former Headmaster Bargoed Grammar School), Mr Islwyn Hughes, Judith Jones. Seated is Mr Illtyd David (President).

156. Heolddu Crescent Carnival 1950-51. From left to right in the back row are Mr Stephens (Cobbler), Mrs Stephens, Audrey Butler (Lady in waiting), Mrs Butler, Mrs E Box, Mrs Edwards, Maureen Sullivan (Lady in waiting), Mr J Box and Mrs B Box. In the centre is carnival queen Maureen Edwards. Front row - Vera Cannon (Flower girl), Gerald Evans (Page boy) and Myrtle Meadow (Flower girl).

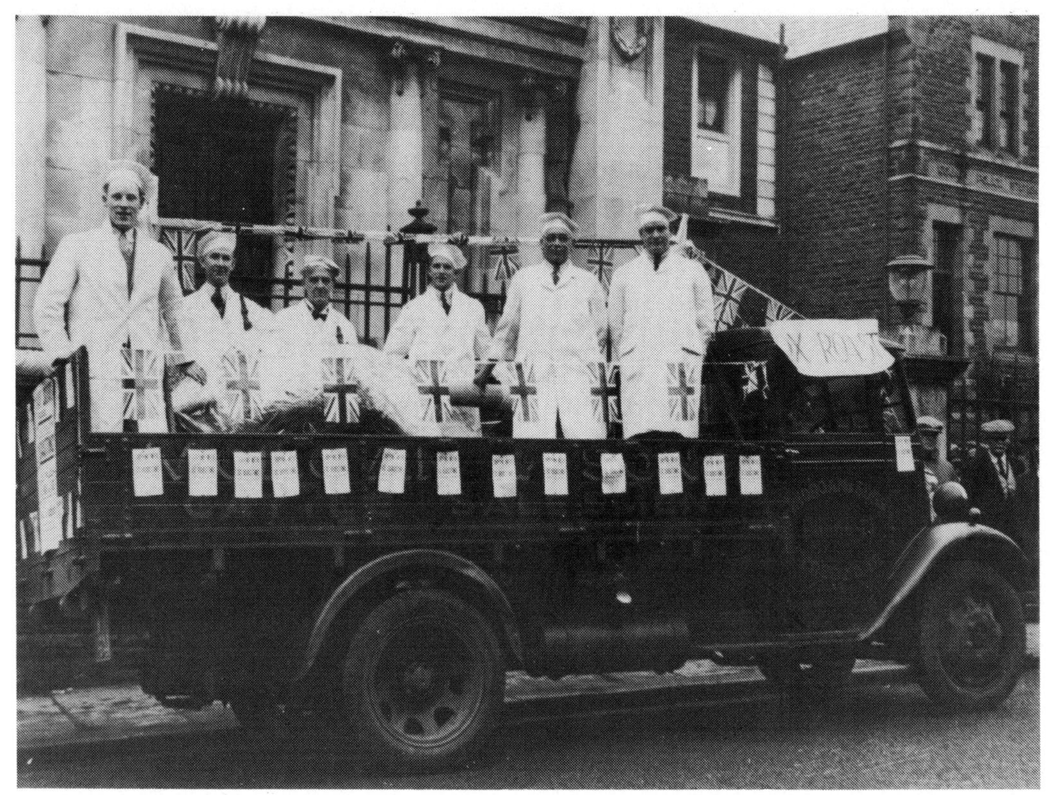

157. Just before the outbreak of the Second World War in 1939 and many years of subsequent food rationing, is this display entitled The Ox Roast. In the background can be seen Bargoed Police Court.

158. A photograph of an unusual event held at the Bargoed Rotary and Round Table Carnival in 1972. A 'piano smashing contest' has just been completed and the participants Graham Turner, John Goldsworthy, Paul James and Mel Winstone take a well-earned rest.

159. Not often does a political dignatory visit the locality and this picture shows the R H George Thomas, the then Secretary of State for Wales, later to become Lord Tonypandy, receiving a Gelligaer tie from Council Chairman Mr Turner. The event took place at a dinner held at the Institute in 1969.

160. From the 1920s can be seen an outing by charabanc, complete with solid rubber tyres. Aboard are parents and children of Llewellyn Street and Railway Terrace, Gilfach off to the seaside for the day.

161. Are there any readers who can remember the roller skating rink at Bargoed? It was situated near the railway station and the photograph shown here is of the resident band in the year 1915.

162. The Second World War affected many a way of life, never to be the same again. This picture shows the last Bargoed Emporium Staff Ball, held in 1939 and a presentation night for Mrs G W Davies.

163. The First World War started in August 1914 and lasted until November 1918. There was no conscription at first and the call from the military leadership echoed those immortal words 'Your Country Needs You!' Above is a rare photograph of the recruiting office set up in Bargoed with a batch of volunteers ready to go to the 'Front'.

164. The Second World War ended in Europe in May 1945 and the country celebrated with street parties galore. This was the scene at West Street marking the event.

165. Members of the Bargoed Police Force in years gone by are seen left to right, back row - L Kiff, R Evans, G Davies, F Wicks, W Willis, L Price, K Powell and G Winfield. Front row - J Davies, M Hopkins, Dot Edwards, G Coslett, B Rees, D Lewis and M Rees.

166. Dutiful members of the local Fire Service when the station was in Gilfach Street during the 1950s. Left to right can be seen Ned Owens, Trevor Price, Tommy Gelson, Alex Chamberlain, Evan Owens and Clive Warren.

167. The National Fire Service was made up of volunteer men and women during the 1939-1945 war. Of the folk pictured here in 1943, the author has unfortunately not been able to trace the name of the gentleman on the far left but the rest of the crew left to right are - Mervyn Thomas, Nancy Assirati, Mervyn Williams, Beryl Jones and Laura Price.

168. Another interesting photograph taken during the dark days of the Second World War. The smiling faces here are gathered at St Gwladys School which was used as a first aid post in 1940.

169. Outside Gilfach Presbyterian Church Llewellyn Street for the Festival of Britain in 1951. Some of the faces to be seen are Allen Bye, Colin Hancox, Lawson Hancox, Billy Lambe, Joyce Hancox, Ron Hancox, Dolly Hancox, Cliff Webb, Lou Carter, Hannah Welch, Jim Welch, Alan Hellyer, Betty Webb, Cliff Webb, Jack Pritchard, Mr & Mrs Frank Richards, Shirley Kennersly, Steve Johns and Margaret Johns.

170. The onlookers here are pictured whilst applauding the local carnival at Gilfach in 1978.

171. Readers are asked to study this collection of local faces and try putting some names to them. The group is pictured on an outing organised by the Cosy Cafe during the 1930s. The cafe was situated next to the former department store of George, Rees and Jones and seated in the centre is Mr Jack Jubilee the cafe owner at the time.

172. This ensemble of characters is pictured in 1921 at Gilfach, probably at an annual carnival and are laying claim to first prize as the Gilfach Jazz Band.

173. Bargoed Cambrian Gleemen 1951. Amongst the faces are L Jenkins (Assistant Pianist), J Harris (Hon Sec), Alan Withers (Vice President), Miss Mavis Rowlands (Accompanist), Griff Hughes (Conductor), Rita Rowlands (Soloist), Mrs Eva Hardy (Vice President).

174. The ladies' section of Gwerthonor Workingmens' Club during the 1970s and a selection of those photographed are Olga Langford, Fay Lerwill, Eileen Wallbank, Iris Shaw, Doreen Saunders, G Williams, F Lewington, D Richards, M Richards, J Curry, L Williams, J Price, S Clabby and I Wallbank.

175. These lads are entrants for a local carnival during the 1950s. Holding the horse is Mr Gwyn Thomas. Two of the boys sat on the cart with blackened faces are Bernard Oliver and John Lemin and stood at the side is Colin Hancox. In the background can be seen Gilfach Presbyterian Church, since demolished.

176. St Margarets Church Hall Pantomime. Left to right, David Honeybun, Ron Wingrove, unknown, Wendy Mullett, Denzil Gough, Mr Wilding, Barbara Davies, Gillian Thomas, Christine Bryant, Linda Williams, unknown, Richard Mullett, Rosalind Beer, unknown, unknown and Malcolm Davies.

177. A flag-lined Greenfield Street at Bargoed sets the scene for a party held during the Festival of Britain celebrations in 1951. Some names are Edna Richards, Glyn Morris, Lily Ray, Allan Morris, Anne Morris, Norma Rawlings, Dolly Smith, Maude Simms (Hairdresser), Fred Mudge, Barbara Powell, May Smith, Irene Collins, Sheila Powell, Leslie Powell, Robert Dunkley, Joan Smith, Carol Smith and Alfred Smith.

178. Not to be left out of any street party activity is Vere Street, Gilfach. Again, memories have faded somewhat but it is thought that the event above was also during the 1951 Festival of Britain. Some of the participants here are Robert Sharp, Dennis Williams, Janet Evans, Adrian Evans, Mrs Doreen Richards, Mrs Rose Price, Mrs Muriel Bell, Mrs Iris Acreman and Mrs Dolly Morgan (the shop).

179. Gilfach Presbyterian Church presents a pantomime 'The Wishing Gnome' which was organised by Mrs Sarah Deneen seen on the far left. Among the cast also to be seen are - Janet Evans, Joan Price, Joy Morgan, Beverly Walters, Glyn Morgan, Bernard Oliver, Brian Ashcroft, Malcolm Bridgway, Lesley Bridgway, Colin Hancox, Ron Hancox, Joyce Hancox, Pat Lambe and Keith Hancox.

180. The ladies' section of Gilfach Workingmens' Club who gave a Christmas performance of The Black and White Minstrels during the 1970s. Top row, left to right - Cora Jones, Pat Lewis, Gwladys Davies, Eileen Chard, Phylis Yeo, Megan Lynch and Beat Boulton. Front row - Jane James, Brenda Fox, Diane Davies, Marion Wright, unknown, May Watkins and Irene Davies.

181. Gilfach OAP outing to Blackpool in the 1970s. Among those to be seen are Marie Morgan, Annie Watkins, Eileen Wallbank, Harold Cobb, Jack Mathews, Bessie Jones, Betty Knight, Jack Knight, Chris Mathews, Billy Edmunds, Mr & Mrs Jim Watkins, Mrs Mary Woods and Mrs Muriel Rees.

182. With almost a hundred voices, seen here is the Bargoed Powell Duffryn Choir in the 1930s.

183. Many readers will recall the celebrations in May 1995 marking the 50th Anniversary of V E Day. Above is a photograph from the original event to mark the end of the war in Europe in May 1945 and some of those present at Vere Street are - Kitty Pember, Valerie Pember, Rose Price, Ralph Watkins, a very young Tudor Davies, Iris Price, Jack Mathews, Thelma Price and Mrs Sarah Deneen.

184. This picture of Gilfach Carnival at Gwerthonor Place was taken in 1978 so the children seen here would be adults now and might have fun recognising themselves. Among those here are Michelle Wilmot, Jacqueline James (Welsh lady) and Caroline James (the matchbox).

185. Llewellyn Street Carnival. The two horses are Beauty and Kitty owned by William David Thomas (known as Thomas the Stick as he chopped and sold stick around the village), some names have been put to the faces shown and these are William Thomas, Gwyn Thomas, Maggie Oliver, Doreen Rice, Mrs Blewitt, Hazel Rice, Gwyneth Jenner, David Carter, Ruth Thomas, Dolly Carter, John Ashcroft, Cyril Weaver, Beryl Butland, Jean Jenner, Marion Bradbury, Mavis Butland, Lynne Davies, Christine Rice, Brian Ashcroft, Mr Butland, Mrs Jenner and Mrs Flew.

186. In the dark economic times of the 1930s, a day trip to Barry Island was considered a luxury. Among the lucky daytrippers from Gilfach seen here in 1936 are - Mrs Eirwen Davies, Mrs Mary Davies, Cyril Watkins, Mrs Annie Watkins, Mrs Elizabeth Chinnock, Betty Chinnock, Pamela Watkins, Dorcas Davies, Harriet Davies, John Davies, Lynette Davies, Lily Pocknell and Gwyneth Davies.

CHAPTER 5

Sport and Recreation

187. There is uncertainty regarding this picture but it does appear to be an athletic event of some importance judging by the crowds at Trafalgar Square, probably during the 1930s. The only person known by name at the front is Mr George Walters.

188. The proud finalists of Gilfach in a 1950-51 soccer season and left to right are, back row - Mr Burrows, D Pinney, K Thomas, J Allen, J B Morgan, G Lewis, G Morgan and L Jones. Front row - E Jones, R Hancox, K Davies, D Williams and J Wallbank.

189. From earlier years, the 1924-25 season Gilfach Albions pose for a photograph with a fine trophy. Back row, left to right - J Griffin (Treasurer), C Camisa, T Turner, E Holifield, T Kingsley, R Edmunds, T Brownett, T Powell and R Tugwell (Trainer). Middle row - B King (Secretary), ? Cowles, A Gibson, G E Greenman (Chairman), W Roberts, J Wallbank and W Jones. Front row - C Thompson, L Thompson (Captain), A Thompson and W Powell.

190. A soccer 'eleven' calling themselves the Bargoed Stars with some supporters in the Park in 1921.

191. Bargoed Thursdays AFC. Rhymney Valley League and Cup Winners 1934-1935. Back row, left to right - T Kennersley, C Lewis, G Matthews, C Evans, W Edwards (Vice Captain), D Wallbank, W Jones, S Davies (Secretary) and D Rawlings (Treasurer). Front row - E Jones (Trainer), S Shide, G Assarati, H Peters (Captain), W Williams (Secretary), I Powell and G Thomas.

192. Gilfach YMCA Football Team when they were Rhymney Valley League Champions 1949-50. Back row, left to right - J Williams, C B Best, J Stuckley, L Evans, P Maher, R Davies, K Goodenough and C Harding. Second row - G Ashcroft, B Board, T Harding, A Andrews, F Rice and R Davies. Front row - J Thomas and W Jones.

193. A late 1960s Gilfach YMCA Football Team. Back row, left to right - G Davies, B Jones, C Thomas, G David, R Jenkins, R Tucker, W Dainton, R Bishop, B Horsman and H Andrews. Front row - B Reynolds, D Humphries, G Davies, P James (Mascot), B Stenner, S Sanger and J Pickett.

194. Ready for the 'off' are these supporters of Wales on their social club outing from Bargoed to Ireland in 1958. To be seen are, back row, left to right - L Martin, N Wilcox, unknown, A Roberts, D Edwards, B Jones, I Jones, R Thomas and D Evans. Middle row - F Mudge, E Roberts, L Ford, B Jones, R Bayliss, unknown, R Evans, W Evans, C Jones and A Frayling. Front row - B Williams, W Boobyer, T Jerimiah, T Edwards, R Pearce, A Smith, S Jones, C Young and E Foster.

195. Bargoed Royals Football Team Rhymney Valley League Cup Winners 1937-38. Back row, left to right - F Davies (Secretary), G Matthews, R Davies (Committee) and J Roberts (Trainer). Middle row - E Davies (Committee), R Morgan (Committee), L Thomas, D Chandler, W Roberts, G Rees, T J Smith (League Secretary) and T Willetts (Treasurer). Front row - J Sage (League Chairman), R Rees, T Rees, J Farmer (Captain), H Morgan (League President), A Lewis, W Willetts and S Bowen (S W M A).

196. Bargoed Pigeon Club with Mr Ken Turner, Chairman of the Council presenting the Investiture Cup donated by the G U D C to Tommy Smart, clocked by Michael Price who had the only bird home in race time. Standing, left to right - D Simmon, S Helps, M Price, S Duggan, S Davies, F Acreman, B Burton, T Smart, R Thomas, T Burgess, B Clarke, K Turner, D Evans, C Smart, C Roberts, B Fowler, B Kendrick, T Hitchman and F Shirley. Sitting - A Morgan and Mr Thomas.

197. The gentle and ancient game of bowls is well supported by the combined clubs of Bargoed and Gilfach, seen here on the 'green' in the 1960s.

198. Some former members of Bargoed Golf Club photographed during the 1950s. Back row, left to right - unknown, H D Riden, Stan Hughes, unknown, unknown, B A Davies, P Rees, McCutchean, L Jenkins, unknown, K McCutchean. Front row - Mr Williams, P G Williams, S James, M Jenkins, D Sallis and Lance Jones. In the centre is Mickey Stanaway.

199. The game of golf is certainly not restricted to the the gentlemen of the locality as witnessed by this fine gathering of players belonging to the Bargoed Golf Club in about 1955.

200. The Gilfach YMCA Basketball Team of 1947-48. Back row, left to right - Renny Davies, John Burgess, John Miles, Joe Stuckey, Des Jones, Elias Evans, Les Bowen and Theo Harding. Front row - Ray Silverthorne, Ken Pearce, Sid Faulkner, Derek Rees (Captain), Vince Trigg, Ray Davies and Phil Maher.

201. The old open air swimming pool, once situated in Bargoed Park. This was closed and the ground converted into a green field play area in the early 1980s.

202. Gilfach Albions Football Team at the rear of the Presbyterian Church 1910. Winners of Division 3 of the Glamorgan League. Back row, left to right - M F Ridge, D O Ridge, A Davies, G Kinsley and B Hancox. Second row - J Llewellyn (Trainer), D Harris, J Smith, D Davies, S Jones and R V Collins (Treasurer). Third row - A Atkinson, W Woodward, H Boxley, T Matthews and S Farmer. Kneeling at front - W Rice and L Price.

203. This Bargoed book is intended to give a wide ranging illustration of the sporting life in the district and not to be missed are these enthusiasts of Gilfach Tennis Club with a fine trophy shield on display.

204. A rather aged photograph, thought to have been taken in 1910 of some Gilfach cricketers. Just a few names are available a Mr Smith (3rd right, back row). Centre are W Mathews, D Davies, unknown and Jess Matthews. In the front row and on the left hand side is Archie Alway.

205. Gilfach YMCA Cricket Team 1948-49. Back row, left to right - V Trigg, K Pearce, J Williams, L Evans, R Silverthorn, J Miles, G Wadman, A Andrews and R Heath. Front row - H Griffiths, A Dando, D Jones, C B Best, R Turner, L Jones and P Maher.

206. Bargoed Grammar School 1st XI Hockey Team during 1951. Back row, left to right - Menna Baker, Marlene Thompson, Gaynor Willetts, Mary Bowen, Marion Evans and Eileen Williams. Front row - Marlene Morgan, Christine Brierley, Marion Currie, Lilian Greenaway, May Navin and Corinne Edwards.

207. Bargoed Grammar School Boys' Athletic Team 1951-52. Standing, left to right - David Davies, Colin Williams, Roger John, Len Evans, David March and Allan Jones. Seated - L Jenkins, H Roberts, B Watkins, A Morgan, G Bosanko and A Cresci. In front - D Goldstein, Clem Watkins and David Morris.

208. Bargoed RFC 1945-46. Back row, left to right - J Jones, B Burgess, A McCarthy, D Harris, L Evans, J Carter, A Edwards, J Evans, D Jones and T Jenkins. Middle row - B Marsden, H Cook, T Probert, G Rawlings, D Evans, T Rees, E Morgan. Front row - P Williams and G Bird.

209. Bargoed North Rugby Team 1951-52. Back row, left to right - B Wall, E Whiting, S Shaw, B Terry, T Hammond, ? Thomas, ? Jones and ? Rogers. Front row - J Chard, P Stockholm, J Cobley, J Wallbank, ? Roberts and D Bowden.

210. Bargoed RFC Centenary Year 1st XV. Back row, left to right - Dr M Sheen, E Jones, L Hill, J Rogers, M Waythe, I Richards, M Jones, A Griffiths, S Powell, W Morgan and J Howells. Middle row - R Lacey, G Webb, M Thomas, M Pratten, B Butcher, R Butcher and J Exton. Front row - G Williams and H Jones.

211. Bargoed RFC Centenary Year Youth XV. Back row, left to right - Dr M Sheen, G Phillips, A Meredith, P Dyer, A Lloyd, N Jones, R Thompson, A Conway, I Williams and S Powell. Front row - G Dainton, D Aldridge, S Wilder, C Jones, S Aldridge, J Williams and A Jones.

212. Bargoed RFC Centenary Year Committee. Back row, left to right - G Williams, J Aldridge, D Carter, R Nelson, A Wadley, H Jones, M Davies, J Maslin, A Hellings and Dr D Williams. Front row - R Clabby, A Lovell, L Powell, I Richard, G Adams, J Muscott, C Milsom and G Ferris.

213. The Bargoed Lilies Rugby Team 1905-06 Season pictured outside The Hanbury Hotel. Back row, left to right - E Jones (Secretary), Mr Phillips (President), E J Blayton (Chairman), T Hancock, B Knibbs, J Prosser, A Phipps, G Carpenter, D Limerick (Treasurer) and P Butler (Linesman). Middle row - W Harding, E Johnson, T Price, A Williams (Captain), T G Fisher, J Jones and T Campbell (Vice-Captain). Front row - A Hutton, J Price and W Hughes.

CHAPTER 6

Bargoed 'Then' and 'Now'

214./215. This small chapter is devoted to a selection of photographs which will help illustrate the significant changes which have taken place over the years. Above is a view of Hanbury Road Bargoed in 1902 and below is a photograph taken from the same spot in 1996.

216./217. The once thriving railway station with passengers galore in 1906 and then ninety years later, a scene of comparative loneliness. Bargoed is luckier than many Welsh towns however, in that is still does have a rail link to other parts.

218./219. The High Street of 1900 when passers-by could stop for a chat in the middle of the road without fear of fast moving motorised traffic. The houses at the far end of the street were demolished to make way for the building of Bank Chambers. Below is that same street almost one hundred years on.

220./221. Above is what must be one of the oldest known photographs of Lower High Street. This particular picture shows the row of old cottages on the left which were pulled down in 1909 to be replaced by the Palace Cinema, now itself of course no longer there. Below is the area as we know it today.

222./223. Upper High Street in 1901, showing the clock tower awaiting completion. The lower photograph and last one in this Bargoed book is a final reminder of how the scenery and pace of life has changed in and around the town.

Acknowledgements

Acknowledgements are due to the undermentioned who kindly loaned their original photographs to add to the author's own collection in the compilation of this book. Sincere apologies are extended to anyone who may have been inadvertently omitted.

Mr H Andrews, Mr A Assirati and Sons, Bargoed Library, Bargoed Rugby Club, Mr M Ball, The late Mr G Bowen, Mrs C Box, Mrs T Cooper, The late Mr G Coslett, Mr D B Faulkner, Mr & Mrs B Horsman, Mrs H Hughes, Mr L Jenkins, Mr & Mrs D Jenner, Mrs C E M Jones, The late Mr W J Lambe, Mr Billy Lambe, Mrs O Langford, Mrs D Lewis, Mrs R Lewis, Mr P Maher, Mrs Valerie Mansell, Mrs A Mullins, Mr R Mullett, Mrs E B Owens, Mr L Powell, Mrs A Prasowski, Mr & Mrs J Ricci, Mr P Richards, Mrs B Rowlands, Mr J Sullivan, Mr J Swattridge, Mr G Thomas, Mr K Turner, Mr J Wallbank, Mrs M Walters, Mr S Walters, Miss J Williams and The late Mrs E Withers.

The author is currently planning a second volume of this book and would very much welcome the loan of any further photographs or material from readers who may wish to see them included. He may be contacted at the address of the publishers.